Arlene

MARLA JAMES- SWANBERG

LifeRich Publishing is a registered trademark of The Reader's Digest Association, Inc.

LifeRich Publishing books may be ordered through booksellers or by contacting:

LifeRich Publishing
1663 Liberty Drive
Bloomington, IN 47403
www.liferichpublishing.com
844-686-9607

Because of the dynamic nature of the Internet, any web addresses or links contained in this book may have changed since publication and may no longer be valid. The views expressed in this work are solely those of the author and do not necessarily reflect the views of the publisher, and the publisher hereby disclaims any responsibility for them.

Any people depicted in stock imagery provided by Getty Images are models, and such images are being used for illustrative purposes only. Certain stock imagery © Getty Images.

ISBN: 978-1-4897-4309-1 (sc)
ISBN: 978-1-4897-4310-7 (e)

Printed in the United States of America.

LifeRich Publishing rev. date: 09/20/2022

My 103-year-old Mom, whose love of Christianity, humor and life will keep you smiling and maybe a little teary until the end.

Contents

Foreword

This book is a labor of love, compiling of many pieces of paper, (some typed, some hand written), scribbled notes, torn out pages of magazines, and note cards that my mom had kept to share. They included jokes, inspirational sayings (that she loved to post on her bedroom door for others to read), funny stories, religious humor, children's sayings, riddles, interesting trivia, and much more. There were so many files and boxes of papers filled with this material that to be honest, I felt so over whelmed with all of this I just thought of disposing of them, but I knew how much time and enjoyment my mom had spent saving and collecting these to share with her friends and family. After much thought, I felt like I really wanted to do something as a tribute to her love of life, her wanting to bring laughs and joy into lives of others, plus some of what I experienced with her through the years, in hopes it will bring some laughter, some inspiration, some learning, some ideas for making get togethers fun, and maybe even some sympathetic tears. This is for you mom, for a life well lived, the love you shared, the inspiration you gave, your many teachings that are still with me, your various talents, the times we shared talking, laughing, and reading. You are no longer here on earth but your light will shine on me until we meet again. Thank you for being my mom and even loving me when I wasn't so loveable. I love you mom and I am so glad, that while you were here, you knew and felt that truth. In life, sooner or later, we all learn that we shouldn't take things for granted. What we cherish today may not be here tomorrow. Invest your time and efforts in the people and things you really love. You will never regret that undertaking.

Chapter 1

The Finality

September 22, 2021, the first day of Fall and my favorite season. Especially after an unusually hot summer, the cooler, fresh air was welcomed. I looked forward to the beautiful change of colors on the trees and becoming a "leaf looker" as we take rides through the countryside admiring those magnificent scenes. Putting planters of colorful mums, along with carved pumpkins and a scarecrow with a bale or two of hay on the front porch, makes the season seem really festive. The coming of Halloween where we see the kids dressed in various costumes was something we also looked forward to. This year it was a sad day for us as it was the day my 103-year-mom died.

I had to call some people to let them know of her passing. That was difficult to do as the reality of it had not quite set in for me. People tried to show comfort which was appreciated. My niece, who had been close to my mom (her grandma) felt like she needed to do something, so she went to the cemetery in Falconer, NY where my dad is buried, and where my mom would join him after her funeral. She called me when she got home and told me that she sat by the gravesite and said, "Grandpa, I just wanted to tell you that your quiet time is over. Grandma will be joining you in a few days." Through my sadness, I laughed for the first time since my mom's passing. Just knowing my dad was a man of little words, and my mom quite the opposite, gave me that needed humor. I knew my mom would have gotten a laugh out of that. It made me feel better because finding some humor in our sadness is just what my mom would have wanted.

Chapter 2

The Beginning

My mom was a big part of my life for the better part of 75 years. I was truly blessed to have her around for that long. Only a small segment of our population gets to experience that amount of time here on earth. What a history she had lived thru during the time she was born. The Depression, the roaring 20's, the World Wars 1 and 2 among some of them, and even being born before women had the right to vote. The current technology advancement was not even imagined in 1918 the year of her birth. Televisions had not been invented, no video games or cell phone were on the scene. Most people today wonder how they did without them. The old saying "you can't miss what you don't have" would be the best answer to that, in my opinion. I was pleasantly surprised with the fact she always tried to keep up with current happenings of the day. She perused the web, read articles and played solitaire besides typing, and copying things she wanted to keep on the computer or in her many files. You had to make yourself remember that this was a 103 yr. old woman.

She was extremely independent, proud, intelligent, strong, talented, funny, and creative. She was widowed at 73 when my dad died of lung cancer. Talk about opposites attract, that definitely was the case with my mom and my dad. He loved and played sports. Even though he was blessed with three daughters, but no sons, we never felt he wanted to trade us in. I really liked school sports and winning the high jump in school and Archery contest for the city, gave me some confidence in sports. I also was a cheerleader for the midget league football team and JR high and High School so I felt I had made a contribution to sports too! My mom loved entertaining her many friends and cared little to watch sports. My dad was eventually inducted into the Hall of Fame in Chautauqua County, NY and, for that, she was really proud of his accomplishment. They had been living in Florida at that time but after the death of my dad, and at age 75, she proceeded to pack her things and move back to New York to her hometown. Isn't that supposed to be the other way around? Not for my mom! She wanted to go back "home."

She lived alone until she was 97 in a two- story house with a basement where she stored many items and did her laundry. My two sisters and I were always concerned about her carrying things up and down stairs. She thought we were being silly. After all she had been line dancing at 95! She drove until she was 97. Her driver's license had a renewal date age of 103! She had three accidents within six months, (she wasn't charged with any of them), but decided that God wanted her to give up her Driver's license. The thought of us having to take the keys away from this extremely independent woman had weighed heavily on us and we silently thanked God for his part in her decision.

Chapter 3

Start of Caregiving

In many ways it was a blessing that she came to live with my husband and I for the last six years of her life. Being a caregiver can be very stressful and learning to give more than you get, and keeping unproductive words and thoughts to yourself, sure helps for more positive days. You have to remember, you are dealing with a person who has for so long made decisions and done things for themselves, and now they have to let go of that independence and pride to accept help from others. So many people have a difficult time with this, including to some degree, my mom. Having to leave your home, give up many of your possessions, can no longer drive, move to another state, is overwhelming for me to even think about. I only can imagine having to do it! We will always be thankful that she could spend her last years in a home with family. I learned so much about the downfalls of being elderly but also about the wisdom of having lived so many years and to appreciate the different stages of life that we go through. Learning that in order to function healthy, we need to adjust our abilities to meet those stages and accept what we can no longer do, and embrace finding new interests and the wisdom we can share with others.

There were day's I would go into my mom's room and I knew she was having a difficult day. She had a lot of Arthritis that had set in her legs and it was difficult for her to walk. She also had lost a lot of her balance and that made it even worse. She pretty much was in constant pain. She refused to take pain pills as she knew they could be addictive. At her age, I don't think I would have worried about that, but she had made up her mind! My mom had been so used to being active and involved in things all of her life, and the loss of this ability was the most difficult for her to accept. I don't think she ever really did. Still, she didn't give up trying to do her best. She got up every day, and dressed herself. She felt that if you gave up, stayed in bed, stopped doing anything, or worst of all stopped caring, that would be the end. She believed God had put her on this earth for a certain amount of time and she would make the best of the time she had left. She would sometimes ask me, "I wonder why God still wants me to be here?" I would try to say something humorous like, "He probably wants you to still keep your eye on me!" She would go back to doing what she could. She talked with her family and friends on the phone and would send them cards where there usually was a funny joke or quote inside to make them smile. The Arthritis in her hands kept her from writing well, but she still made the effort. Her eyes were growing dim and although she had been an avid reader, that was getting much less frequent. We would spend time in the evening where I would read her books we enjoyed. We both enjoyed those times. Many days I would see her trying so hard that I would have to find an excuse to leave her so she wouldn't see my tears. When I don't feel like doing something I know I should, I just think of the efforts my mom had made to finish her tasks, and I straighten up and get going! She would think of procrastination as a form of laziness. I use to tell her there were times I just knew I would do a better job with something tomorrow!

At this stage of her life, and thoughts, it made me think of a prayer she kept in her room that I am sure she read often. The author is unknown and it is titled:

"He Makes No Mistake."

My father's way may twist and turn,
My heart may throb and ache;
But in my soul, I'm glad to know
He makes no mistake.

My cherished plans may go astray,
My hopes may fade away;
But still, I'll trust my Lord to lead,
For he does know the way.

Though night be dark and it may seem
That day will never break,
I'll pin my faith, my all, on him;
He makes no mistake.

There's so much now I cannot see,
My eyesight's far too dim;
But come what may, I'll simply trust
And leave it all to him.

For by and by the mist will lift,
And plain it all He'll make;
Through all the way, though dark to me,
He made not one mistake.

Chapter 4

Decorating Skills

I have to include some of the things that stand out about mom in my memories as I was growing up. I would say that my mom was just ahead of her time. Others would just be taken aback and somewhat overwhelmed by her "daring to be different" projects. But in the end, the majority usually found favor with her creativity. Actually, I remember this at an early age. We did not have a big house and my older sister and I shared a bedroom. My mom wanted to fix it up so we both would like it. One day when we came in from outside, she had us close our eyes and then go into the closet where she proceeded to turn on the light. The room was not big but we did have a pretty large closet and my mom had painstakingly put fairy tale characters on all the walls. There was Snow white and the Seven Dwarfs, Little Red Riding Hood and the wolf, Goldie Locks and Three Bears, Cinderella and her evil step mom and three sisters, Jack in the Beanstalk climbing the stalk, Little BO Peep and her lost Sheep, and the Three Pigs. It was like stepping into a world of fairy tales. That made our room special and my friends loved it. We did not have a lot of money, but we had lots of creativity and humor, thanks to my mom. It made us feel like we had things other kids did not have.

Another example of her creativity was seen when I walked into my parents' bedroom and saw a big black tree painted on the wall above the bed. It had gold leaves painted on it. But it didn't stop there. Gold leaves were painted on the maple head board as though falling from the tree. They proceeded to the dresser where it appeared as though the gold leaves had apparently blown. My mom looked so pleased with her work that I could only smile and say that is "so different!" (Today that would probably be suggested by home decorators and costly!) I immediately wondered what my dad would say but the only thing I ever heard from him was "Hmm, I probably am the only guy that sleeps on a bed with leaves falling around him every night let alone stuck to my dresser!" I was pleasantly surprised that was all he said!

Then there was the time that mom had decided the dining room needed brighter colors. She fixed that dilemma by painting our piano pink. It was an older piano but we had never thought we would see it pink! "Isn't that just what the room needed," she happily said and we just looked at each other. "Well, it did brighten up the room" mom, we all replied!

My dad was the type of person that when he did something, it needed to be done right. Our bathroom needed an update and he painstakingly stripped the wainscot and painted it a bright white. He also painted all the walls. Just the new paint job really made a refreshing difference. While he was at work, my mom thought it would be really unique to add some touches to the walls. She got a can of black paint and wanted my sisters and I to put our hands in the paint and then put our hand prints on the walls. Such a modern touch! Now actually, that might have been unique if the paint hadn't been too thin and ran down the walls and down on the newly painted wainscot. My sisters and I just stared at the mess in dismay and my mom started crying. After all his work, what would my dad say!? When he came home, he walked in the bathroom saw my mom by the bathtub crying, and I think he felt so sorry for her and shocked at what he saw, that he said nothing. He just picked up all the paint splattered newspapers that had been laid down on the floor and started repainting. I always wondered whether he really felt that sorry or he was afraid of what he would say if he opened his mouth. But then again, I guess he loved her enough to forgive her shortcomings. I gave my dad many kudos for his tolerance!

Oh yes, I have to mention our hallway. You know how dark and undecorated they can be according to my mom. Well, she felt that pink polka dots would fix that problem! We came home from school to find big pink circles all over the hall walls and stairway. By now, it wasn't that surprising to find something done new in the house, but that was definitely different. After a while my mom got tired of the circles and thought a new paint job should be undertaken. Of course, being my mom, you can't let a holiday go by without decorating. Since it was nearing Easter, why not take advantage of something you are going to redo anyway? So, we awoke to find rabbit ears, eyes, and whiskers painted on the big pink polka dots! We did get a kick out of that!

You know, again according to my mom, your mailbox should be something people notice, so after some thought, my mom decided that striping would be just the thing. Soon, a rainbow of colors radiated from the road side mail box. You could spot it from quite a distance. People had no problem finding our house. We just had to tell them to watch for the mailbox! I never remember being embarrassed by my mom's undertakings. Again, I just thought she was ahead of her time. Looking at today's décor, I believe I was right.

I do remember her making beautiful arrangements out of dried weeds and flowers that we would pick from the woods and she would paint them. I think those times walking in the woods were some of my favorites. Actually, she was really good at making any arrangement. When she lived with me, I always let her make mine for the holidays. She gave some of her arrangements to friends and I knew that the people who received them felt they were really special.

She took us to the creeks to find stones. We needed to find stones shaped like something. We did, but most of the time it was only the finder that saw the dog, lion, flower or whatever in their stone. My mom must have had a good eye for shapes to find stones that did look like something we all saw. She would paint those, defining the image in the stone, and display them. I still have several of her stones that I have put in planters and even dishes for display. She even taught a rock/stone painting class at her church later in life.

Where we lived in NY, there were wild violets that grew in the woods and fields. My mom, my two sisters and me, would find the old violet growing places that we knew and we would search for new places every Spring. The last two days of April we would pick bunches of them (a rather lengthy process) and divide them into bouquets. My mom would take white paper doilies, cut a hole in the middle of the doily and put the stems through it leaving the flowing part on top. She would tie a purple ribbon around the gathered stems. On May 1, (May Day), we would take the lovely bouquets to neighbors and place them at their doors after ringing the door bell and leaving. They were not supposed to see you leaving the bouquets but I don't think we were very good at hiding! We liked seeing their surprised faces and smiles. We celebrated many May days that way and I know the neighbors looked forward to that gift of beauty and friendship. I am not sure if any people still do that today for May Day, but it taught us that a little kindness goes a long way. Thanks for that lesson of creativity, giving, and kindness, Mom!

My mom also took the time to visit people in several of the nursing homes in our area. She would bring them some of her baked treats or a small gift. She had friends who had to go live there for various reasons so I know they looked forward to her visits. She always brought along a few of her funny stories to share. I would always get a (stifled) laugh out of her coming home and saying "those poor older people. I know they would rather be living in their own homes." At the time, she was in her late 80's and continued well into her 90's. She was older than many of her friends that were living there! It was important to my mom that we show caring to people of all ages while we are still able to. Another really good lesson to pass on to both adults and children

I could go on, but that would take a book in itself and I promised to cover other things.

Chapter 5

Attitudes and Words of Wisdom

My mom had such a positive outlook on life. She experienced the difficult days and times like we all do but she never let the bad times overwhelm her. I really believe that this also had a lot to do with her longevity. Life goes on she would imply and she would find something positive to move forward with setting that goal for all of us. Life is too short to let it bog you down with negativity was something she tried to instill in all of us. I have not mastered that yet, but it is a work in progress. When she lived with me, she loved to post sayings on her bedroom door. They were always good thoughts to think of and everyone who came to visit loved to stop and read them. Maybe we all long to think of uplifting words in times when there are so many things to be down and negative about. I have listed some of the ones she really liked in hopes that they will give you some positive thoughts. Maybe some of you will even get the urge to post them on your door or refrigerator or even your desk at work. You may even find your kids' reading them! Days when you need some positive thoughts, read a few of these again!

"Give every day the chance to become the most beautiful of your life!" – Mark Twain

"Don't dwell on those that get you down, but cherish those that lift you up!" - Anonymous

"Always keep your words short in case you have to eat them! – Andy Rooney

"Don't let yesterday use up too much of today!" – Will Rogers

"You can't be a sharp cookie with a crummy attitude!" – John C. Maxwell

"Worry is wasting today's time to clutter up tomorrow's opportunities with yesterday's troubles!" - Anonymous

"Nothing can make you happy unless you are happy with yourself!"- Anonymous

"A day without laughter is a day wasted!" – Charlie Chaplin

"Don't talk unless you can improve the silence!" – Jorge Luis Borges

"Happiness is an inside job!" – William Arthur Ward

"Be the person that makes someone smile today!" - Anonymous

"Never put both feet in your mouth at the same time because then you won't have a leg to stand on!" - Anonymous

"Accept that some days you are the pigeon and some days you are the statue!" – Scott Adams

"You may be only one person in the world but you may be the world to one person!" – Maulik Pathak

"Nobody cares if you can't dance, just get up and dance!" – Martha Graham

"A truly happy person is one who can enjoy the scenery on an unexpected detour!" - Anonymous

"Be careful how you think, your life is shaped by your thoughts!" – Rick Warren

"What happens outwardly in your life is not as important as what happens inside you!" – Rick Warren

"We could learn a lot from crayons. Some are sharp, some are dull. Some have weird names and they all are different colors, but they all have to live in the same box!" – Robert Fulghum

"A real friend is one who walks in when the rest of the world walks out!" – Walter Winchell

"True friendship is like sound health; the value of it is seldom known until it is lost!" – Charles Caleb Colton

"Strangers are just friends waiting to happen!" – Rod McKuen

"If you can't see the bright side of life, polish the dull side!"- Christina Dodd

"Watch your thoughts; they become words. Watch your words; they become actions. Watch your actions; they become habits. Watch your habits; they become character. Watch your character; it becomes your destiny!" – Frank Jackson

"Keep your face looking toward the sunshine and the shadows will fall behind you!" – Walt Whitman

"Life is like an onion. You peel off one layer at a time and sometimes you weep!" – Carl Sandburg

"Be sure your brain is in gear before engaging your mouth!" - Anonymous

"Find an aim in life before you run out of ammunition!" – Arnold Glasow

"A house is no home unless it contains food for the soul as well as the body!" – Benjamin Franklin

"Happiness is like a butterfly. The more you chase it, the more it will elude you. But if you turn your attention to other things, it comes and softly sits on your shoulder!" – Henry David Thoreau

"The past cannot be changed; the future is still in your power!" - Anonymous

"The real art of conversation is not only to say the right thing at the right time, but also to leave unsaid the wrong thing at the tempting moment!" – Lady Dorothy Nevill

"You can't keep trouble from coming, but you never give it a chair to sit on!" - Anonymous

"Good manners and soft words have brought many a difficult thing to pass!" – Sir John Vanbrugh

"Life is a miracle—and the right to live is a gift!" – Albert Einstein

"Observe the postage stamp; its usefulness depends upon its ability to stick to one thing until it gets there!" – Henry Shaw

"If you outgo exceeds your income, then your upkeep will be your downfall!" – Bill Earle

"To belittle is to be little!" – Khalil Gibran

"It's not the load that breaks you down, it's the way you carry it!" – Lou Holtz

"Learn as if you were to live forever; live as if you were to die tomorrow!" – Mahatma Gandhi

"A minute of thought is worth more than an hour of talk!" – John C. Maxwell

"Learn from the mistakes of others—you can't live long enough to make them all by yourself!" – Eleanor Roosevelt

"Enthusiasm is infectious—and so is the lack of it!" – Dale Carnegie

"A man should never be ashamed to say he has been wrong, which is but saying, in other words, that he is wiser today than he was yesterday!" – Alexander Pope

"A wise woman once said to me, "There are only two lasting bequests we can hope to give our children. One of these is roots, the other, wings!" – Henry Ward Beecher

"A measure of a man's real character is what he would do if he knew he would never be found out!" – Thomas Babington Macaulay

"The sun is up and you are alive—start there!" - Anonymous

"Stars don't shine without darkness!" – D.H. Sidebottom

"You can complain that rose bushes have thorns or rejoice that those thorn bushes have roses!" – Abraham Lincoln

"To speak kindly does not hurt the tongue!" - Proverb

"When your past calls, don't answer. He has nothing new to say!" – Lionel Richie

"No one ever injured their eyesight by looking on the bright side!" - Anonymous

"How do you spell love? You don't spell it, you feel it!" - Anonymous

"Any time you have an opportunity to make a difference in this world and you don't, then you are wasting your time on Earth!" – Roberto Clemente

"Success is getting what you want. Happiness is wanting what you get!" – Dale Carnegie

"Cry, forgive and move on—Let your tears water the seeds of your future happiness!"- Steve Maraboli

"Begin each day with a grateful heart!"- Anonymous

"Swallowing pride is nonfattening!" – Frank Tyger

"You only live once--false---you live every day. You only die once"! – Dwight Schrute

"You are braver than you believe. Stronger than you seem. Smarter than you think and loved more than you know!" – A.A. Milne

"Every day is a new beginning--take a deep breath, smile and start again!" - Anonymous

"Sometimes later becomes never—do it now!" - Anonymous

"Nothing lasts forever. We must master the art of letting go!" - Unknown

"You only fail when you stop trying! - Unknown

"If you want rainbows, you'll have to put up with the rain!" – Dolly Parton

"It only takes one person to change your life—YOU!" - Unknown

"Jumping for joy is good exercise!" - *Unknown*

"Not all storms come to disrupt your life -some come to clear you path!" - *Unknown*

"Don't lose yourself in the search for acceptance by others!" - *Unknown*

"Each day is a new blessing. Let go of all the worries and be grateful for all the positives in your life!" - *Unknown*

"The greatest act of faith somedays is simply getting up and facing another day!" – *Amy Gatliff*

"Happiness is like jam. You can't spread even a little bit without getting some on yourself!" - *Unknown*

"We can't control the world around us but we can control how we respond to it!" – *L. Lionel Kendrick*

"You can't go back and unscramble the egg!" – *J.P. Morgan*

"New Days, New thoughts, New Strength, and New Possibilities!" – *Eleanor Roosevelt*

"It takes such a little effort to smile. Just turn the corners of your mouth up instead of down!" - *Unknown*

"When life throws you many rainy days, play in the puddles!" - *Unknown*

"Be careful of another's feelings!" - *Unknown*

"Pay no attention to ill-natured remarks!" - *Unknown*

"Never let an opportunity pass to say a kind word. Praise good work regardless of who does it!" – *Ann Landers*

"Into the house where joy lives, happiness will gladly come!" – Japanese Proverb

'The best way to remember your wife's birthday is to forget it once!" – Herbert V. Prochnow

"Your ulcers are not due to what you are eating but to what's eating you." - Unknown

"He who dies with the most toys is still dead!" - Anonymous

"It is all right to sit on your pity pot every now and again. Just be sure to flush when you are done!" – Debbie Macomber

"A grudge is a heavy thing to carry!" - Unknown

"Blessed are the flexible as they shall not be bent out of shape!" – Robert Ludlum

"Good is long remembered; bad even longer!" - Anonymous

"If you always do what you have always done, you will always be what you have always been!" – Tony Robbins

"Great minds discuss ideas, average minds discuss events, small minds discuss people!" – Eleanor Roosevelt

"A cynic is someone who knows the price of everything and the value of nothing!" – Oscar Wilde

"It doesn't matter how slowly you go as long as you do not stop!" – Confucius

"If you have never failed, you have never lived!" – Abraham Lincoln

"The truth may hurt for a little while but a lie hurts forever!" - Anonymous

"A heart full of joy is better than a fist full of coins!" – Matshona Dhliwayo

"Falling down is an accident. Staying down is your choice!" - Anonymous

"A bad habit is like a comfortable bed, easy to get into but hard to get out of!" - Anonymous

"You can't climb the ladder to success with your hands in your pocket!" – Arnold Schwarzenegger

"Do what is right, not what is easy!" – Roy T. Bennett

"Anger is only one letter short of danger!" – Eleanor Roosevelt

"The tongue weighs practically nothing, but few people can hold it!" - Nitya Prakash

"Don't wait for the perfect moment but make the moment perfect!" – Aryn Kyle

With all these, I know you'll find many quotes positive reminders and life suggestions. Almost every day, we can find uplifting advice to be reminded of. I know that is why my mom posted these for guests to read.

I will end this section with a saying that I found in my mom's many papers of thoughts because she used this philosophy most of her life and I am sure she would like to pass this on.

"Worry is a total waste of time. IT DOESN'T CHANGE ANYTHING. All it does is steal your joy and keep you busy doing nothing!" - Anonymous (Personally, I think that is worth posting somewhere!)

Chapter 6

Funny Stories, Quotes, and Riddles

My mom loved humor including jokes, quotes, and riddles. She believed everyone needed laughter in their lives to be healthy and happy. She shared old ones and new ones with my husband and I. Since we were the only ones in the house-hold we became her "testers." If we laughed at them, they passed her test to share! For Christmas the year she turned 100, she made creative booklets filled with funny quotes and jokes to send to her friends for a special gift from her. She got many positive responses from the recipients. It took her many hours to make and put those together. I would see how tired she was some days and told her to take a break for a few days. But she was determined to get those done. She many times would say that maybe she wouldn't have a tomorrow. I guess when, and if, you reach that age, that would be a constant thought. It made me feel sad when she said that but I had to admit that was a reality. She finally let me help her put some of the booklets together but she really wanted to do it by herself. It ended up being eight pages and she made 75 to send. It really was a work of love. I will share some of these quotes and jokes with you and hope you will find some laughter as my mom so wanted to pass on. If you were a recipient of one of her booklets, some of these will be familiar to you. I would like to put a disclaimer in here. As, I have stated, I found these quotes and funny stories among her papers and have not been able to find some original authors. I would love to give them the credit and tell them how much she enjoyed the humor and sharing of them with her friends and family.

"My mind works like lightning. One brilliant flash and it is gone!" - Anonymous

"The only time the world beats a path to your door is if you are in the bathroom!" - Anonymous

"After eating an entire bull, a mountain lion felt so good he started roaring. He kept it up until a hunter came along and shot him. The moral: When you are full of bull, keep your mouth shut! – Will Rogers

"Blessed is he who expects nothing, for he shall never be disappointed!" – Alexander Pope

"Never slap a man who is chewing tobacco!" – Will Rogers

"It is extremely important to have a twinkle in your wrinkle!" - Anonymous

"Smile while you still have your teeth!" - Anonymous

"When you find yourself in a hole, the first thing to do is to stop digging!" – Tammara Webber

"It doesn't take a genius to spot a goat in a flock of sheep!" – Will Rogers

"A husband is someone who, after taking out the trash, gives you the impression he just cleaned the whole house!" - Anonymous

"If the shoe fits, buy it in every color?" – Jerry Smith

"Chocolate…Coffee…Men. Some things are just better rich!" - Anonymous

"A penny saved is a government overlook!" – Benjamin Franklin

"Age is a number and mine is unlisted!" - Anonymous

"You know you are getting old when the candles cost more than the cake!" – Bop Hope

"Swallowing your pride occasionally will never give you indigestion!" - Anonymous

"Life is uncertain, eat dessert first!" – Ernestine Ulmer

"When all is said and done, there is a lot more said than done!" - Aesop

"If you don't like the way you were born, try being born again!" - Anonymous

"If you think nobody cares, try missing a couple of payments!" – Earl Wilson

"Inside some of us is a thin person is struggling to get out, but they can usually be sedated with a few pieces of chocolate!" - Unknown

"Adam and Eve had an ideal marriage. He didn't have to hear about all the men she could have married, and she didn't have to hear about the way his mother cooked!" - Unknown

"A clean tie attracts the soup of the of the day!" – Paul Dickson

"It isn't how busy you are, but why you are busy—the bees are praised, the mosquitoes are swatted!" – Marie O'Conner

"My greatest accomplishment is just keeping my mouth shut!" - Unknown

"A computer is almost human, except it does not blame its mistakes on another computer!" - *Unknown*

"Before you give someone a piece of your mind, be sure you can spare it!" - *Unknown*

"It is hard to soar with eagles when you are surrounded by turkeys!" – *Adam Sandler*

"A diplomat is a man that can convince his wife she looks frumpy in diamonds and fat in a mink coat!" - *Unknown*

"To handle yourself, use your head; to handle others, use your heart!" – *Eleanor Roosevelt*

"I'm trying to lose weight but it keeps finding me!" - *Unknown*

Speaking of weight, "One of life's mysteries is how a two- pound box of candy can make a woman gain five pounds!" - *Unknown*

"It is hard to understand how a cemetery can raise its burial costs and blame it on the higher cost of living!" - *Unknown*

"Some people try to turn back their odometers. Not me. I want people to know why I look this way. I've traveled a long way and some of the roads weren't paved!" – *Will Rogers*

"All I want is peace, love, understanding, and a chocolate bar!" - *Anonymous*

"You will always be my friend—you know too much!" - *Unknown*

"The trouble with some women is that they get all excited over nothing and the they marry him!" - *Cher*

"It's ok if you don't like me—everyone doesn't' have good taste!" - *Unknown*

"Better to be over the hill than under it!" - *Unknown*

"Always forgive your enemies, nothing annoys them as much!" – *Oscar Wilde*

"You're not fat you are just easier to see!" - *Unknown*

"Families are like fudge......mostly sweet, with a few nuts!" – *Les Dawson*

"The hardest thing in life to learn is which bridge to cross and which to burn!" – *David Russell*

"Many people will walk in and out of your life. But only true friends will leave footprints on your heart!" – *Eleanor Roosevelt*

"I dream of a better world where a chicken can cross the street without having his motives questioned!" - *Unknown (I love this one too!)*

"Don't take life too seriously —you will never get out of it alive, anyhow!" – *Elbert Hubbard*

"He is nice to people and animals, but you should hear him talk to a golf ball!" - *Unknown*

"There is a new margarine on the market. It's called Rumor because it spreads so fast!" – *Unknown*

"One day two elderly women were eating breakfast together when Bertha noticed something funny in Jeans ear. Jean, do you know that you have a suppository in your right ear? I have a suppository in my right ear she asked in amazement?" She took it out and stared at it.

"Oh, Jean I am so glad you noticed this she exclaimed, now I know where to find my hearing aid!"

"A couple were not talking as they drove through the countryside. They had an argument earlier and neither one wanted to concede their view points. As they passed a farm that had a pen of pigs, goats, and mules, the husband turned toward his wife and sarcastically asked if they were relatives of hers? "Why yes," replied the wife without hesitation, "In-laws!"

"A woman goes with her husband to the Doctor's office. The Doctor does the husband's check-up and asks to take the wife aside to talk with her. "If you do not do the following, your husband is going to die." 1. Each morning you need to fix him a healthy breakfast and have him leave the house in a good mood as he goes off to work. 2. Make him a nutritious lunch and put him in good frame of mind before he goes back to work. 3. For dinner make an especially nice meal and do not ask him to do any household chores. 4. Have sex with him several times a week and satisfy all his needs." On the way home, the husband asked his wife what the Doctor had told her. To which she replied, "you're going to die!"

"The young husband wrote home from his new job saying "made foreman today, a feather in my cap!" A few weeks later he wrote "made Super-intendant today, another feather in my cap!" Some weeks later he wrote again saying, "fired today, send train fare!" Wife wrote back saying, use feathers and fly home!"

"The teacher asked a student what was the chemical formula for water? The student answered H I J K L M N O. "No said the teacher, I do not understand why you would think that." "Well, said the student, yesterday you said it was H to O!"

"Sitting on the side of the highway waiting to catch speeding drivers, a State Police Officer sees a car puttering along at 22MPH, he thinks

to himself, "this is as dangerous as a speeder!" So, he turns on his lights and pulls the driver over. Approaching the car, he notices there are five older ladies—two in the front seat and three in the back—wide eyed and white as ghosts!" The driver obviously confused, says to him, "Officer, I do not understand, I was doing the exact speed limit!" "What's the problem?" "Ma'am" the Officer replied, "you weren't speeding but you should know that driving slower than the speed limit can also be a danger to other drivers." "Slower that the speed limit? No sir, I was doing the exact speed limit—twenty-two miles an hour!" The State Police Officer, trying to contain a chuckle explains to her that "22" was the route number, not the speed limit. A bit embarrassed the woman grinned and thanked the officer for pointing out her error of thinking the route signs were speed limits. "But before I go, Ma'am, I have to ask, is everyone in the car alright? These women seem awfully shaken and they haven't uttered a single peep this whole time." "Oh, they'll be all right in a minute officer. We just got off route 119."

"A husband read an article about how many more words women use a day—30,000 to a man's 15,000. The wife replied, "The reason has to be because we have to repeat everything to men." The husband then turned to his wife and asked, "What?"

"An elderly couple was driving across the country. The woman was driving when she got pulled over by the Highway patrol. "Madam did you know you were speeding?" Being somewhat hard of hearing, she asked her husband "What did he say?" she asked her husband?" The husband told her, "He said you were speeding." The patrolman said, "may I have your license?" "What did he say" she again asked her husband?" "He wants to see your license, the husband replied." The patrolman said "I see you are from Arkansas." I spent some time there and on a blind date, my date was one of the ugliest women I had ever seen." The woman turned to her husband again and asked, "What did he say?" The old man yelled, "he thinks he knows you!"

31

"After dying in a car crash, three friends go to heaven for orientation. They are all asked the same question. "When you were in the casket, and friends and family were mourning over you, what would you have liked to hear them say about you?" The first guy immediately responds, "I would have liked to have heard that I was one of the greatest doctors of my time, and a great family man." The second guy says, "I would have liked to have heard I was a wonderful husband and school teacher who made a huge difference in the lives of our children of tomorrow." The last guy thinks a minute and replies, "I would have liked to have heard them say—LOOK HE'S MOVING!"

"A certain man had invited his pastor and wife for dinner, and it was little Joey's job to set the table. But when it came time to eat, Joey's mother said with surprise and a little embarrassment, "Why didn't you give Mrs. Brown a knife and a fork Joey?" "I didn't think I needed to," Joey explained. "I heard daddy say she always eats like a horse!"

"One morning a man returns after several hours of fishing and decides to take a nap. Although not familiar with the lake, the wife decides to take the boat out. She motors a short distance, anchors, and reads her book. Along came a game warden in his boat. "Good morning, Ma'am. What are you doing?" "Reading a book," she replies, (thinking isn't it obvious?) "You're in a restricted area," he informs her. I'm sorry officer, but I am not fishing, I'm reading." "Yes, but you have all the equipment. For all I know you could start any moment. I'll have to take you in and write you up." "If you do that, I'll have to charge you with sexual assault," says the woman. "But I haven't even touched you," says the Game Warden. "That's true, but you have all the equipment. For all I know you could start at any moment." "Have a nice day, Ma'am," and he left!"

"One evening a husband thinking he was being funny, said to his wife, "perhaps we should start washing your clothes in slim fast. Maybe that *would take a few inches off your butt." His wife was not amused and decided that such a comment could not go by the wayside. The next morning the husband takes a pair of shorts out of his drawer—"what the heck is this?" he says to himself as a cloud of white dust appeared when he shook them out. "Alice" he hollers into the bathroom. "Why did you put talcum powder in my underwear?" She replied with a snicker, "It's not talcum powder, its Miracle Grow!"*

"Susie's husband had been slipping in and out of a coma for several months. Things looked grim, but she was by his side every day. One day as he slipped back into consciousness, he motioned for her to come close to him. She pulled the chair to the bed and leaned her ear close so she would be able to her him. "You know" he whispered, his eyes filling with tears, "you have been with me through all the bad times. When I got fired you stuck right with me. When my business went under, there you were. When my health went down-hill, you still have stayed with me. And do you know what?" "What dear?" she asked gently, smiling to herself." "I think you are bad luck!"

"A man sprawled across three entire seats in a theater. When the usher came by and noticed this, he whispered to the man, "sorry sir, but you're only allowed one seat." The man groaned but didn't budge. The usher became more impatient. "Sir if you do not get up from there, I'm going to have to call the manager." The man just groaned. The usher marched briskly back up the aisle and, in a moment, he returned with the manager. Together the two of them tried repeatedly to move the man, but with no success. Finally, they summoned the police. The Cop surveyed the situation briefly then asked, "All right buddy, what's your name?" "Sam," the man moaned. "Where are ya' from Sam?" With pain in his quivering voice Sam replied, "the balcony!"

"A loaded mini-van pulled into the only remaining campsite. Four children leaped from the vehicle and began feverishly unloading gear and setting up the tent. The boys rushed to gather the firewood, while *the girls and their mother set up the camp stove and cooking utensils. A nearby camper marveled to the youngsters' father, "that sir, is some display of teamwork." The father replied, "I have a system. No one goes to the bathroom until the camp is set up!" (Oh, I would be in big trouble being a part of that team!)*

"A Doctor was home for the evening when he got a phone call. When he answered the call a familiar voice of a colleague was on the end of the line. "We need a fourth player tonight said the friend." "I'll be right over" whispered the Doctor. As he was putting on his coat his wife asked "Is it serious?" "Oh yes, quite serious the Doctor said gravely. In fact, three doctors are already there!"

"A wealthy man was on death's door but wanted to take all his money with him when he died. He asked three of his friends if each would take a share of his money and throw it in the coffin just before it was closed. When the man died a short time later, the three friends threw in the money entrusted to them. After the funeral, the three friends were discussing the service and their part in it. One man confided, "I did a terrible thing." I only threw in half of the money he gave me." Another friend said "I'm guilty too." I only threw in one third of the money he entrusted to me." The third friend exclaimed, "Shame on both of you! I threw in the whole thing making out a check for the full amount!"

"Two women met for the first time since graduating from High School. One asked the other, "You were so organized in school. Did you manage a well-planned life?" "Yes, said her friend. My first marriage was to a millionaire, my second was to an actor, my third was to a preacher, and now I am married to an undertaker." Her friend smiled and asked what that had to do with a well-planned life? "Well, said her friend, one for the money, two for the show, three to get ready, and four to go!"

34

"*John invited his mother over for dinner. During the meal, his mother couldn't help but notice how attractive and shapely the housekeeper was. Over the course of the evening, she started to wonder if there was more between John and the housekeeper than met the eye. Reading his mom's thoughts, John volunteered, "I know what you must be thinking, but I assure you, my relationship with my housekeeper is purely professional." About a week later, the housekeeper came to John and said, "Ever since your mother came to dinner, I've not been able to find that beautiful gravy ladle. You don't suppose she took it do you?" John said, "Well I doubt it but I will write her a letter just to be sure." So, he sat down and wrote: "Dear mother, I'm not saying you did take a gravy ladle from my house, and I not saying you did not take a gravy ladle. But the fact remains that one has been missing since you were here for dinner." Several days later, John received a letter back from his mother. "Dear Son, I am not saying you do sleep with your housekeeper and I am not saying you do not sleep with your housekeeper. But the fact remains that if you were sleeping in your own bed, you would have found the gravy ladle by now!"*

"*Three sisters, 92, 94, and 96 years old respectively, all lived together. One day the oldest drew a bath. She put one foot in the water, paused and then called downstairs to her sisters. "Am I getting in or out of the tub?" The middle sister started up the stairs to help and called back downstairs. "Was I going up or coming down the stairs?" The youngest sister was sitting at the kitchen table having tea said, "I guess I have to go help them, but I hope I never get that forgetful," and then knocked on the wood table. She gets up then pauses and calls out, "I'll come as soon as I see who is at the door!"*

Chapter 7

More Humor from Mom's Papers

Because my mom had collected so many thoughts, quotes, and jokes through the years, obviously good, funny and happy thoughts meant a lot to her. I found a poem she had saved by Mark Twain that stated "Extra thoughts to take along." The name was "A Little More and a Little Less." I know she would have liked me to share it.

"A little more kindness and a little less greed;"

"A little more giving and a little less need;"

"A little more smile and a little less frown;"

"A little less kicking a man when he's down;"

"A little more "we" and a little less "I;"

"A little more laugh and a little less cry."

"A few more flowers along the way of life and fewer on graves at the end of our strife."

Those are thoughts we can all put into practice. Maybe that is the formula we need for a much better world!

"While shopping in a grocery store, two Catholic sisters happen to walk by the beer and wine section. One asked the other if she would like a beer. The second good Catholic sister answered that, indeed, it would be very nice to have one, but that she would feel uncomfortable purchasing it. The first sister replied that she would handle that without a problem. She picked up the six pack and took it to the cashier. The cashier had a surprised look so the good Catholic sister said, "This is for washing our hair." Without blinking an eye, the cashier reached under the counter and put a package of pretzel sticks in the bag with the beer. With a smile on his face he stated, "The curlers are on me!"

"There was a $20 dollar bill and a $1 dollar bill on the conveyor belt at the downtown Federal Reserve Building. As they were laying side, by side, the $1 dollar bill said to the $20 dollar bill, "Hey man, where have you been? I haven't seen you for a long time!" The $20 dollar bill replied, "Man I have been having a ball! I've been traveling to distant countries, going to the finest restaurants, to the biggest and best casinos, numerous boutiques, the mall uptown, the mall downtown, the mall across town and even a mall I helped newly build. "In fact, just this week I've been to Europe, a professional NBA game, Rodeo Drive, and all-day retreat spa's, the top-notch hair salons and the new casino. I have done it all!" After describing his great travels, the $20 dollar bill asked the $1 dollar bill, "What about you?" Where have you been?" The $1 dollar replied, "Well, I've been to the Baptist church, the Methodist church, the Presbyterian church, the Episcopalian church, the Church of God, the Catholic and Mormon churches and the church of the Latter Day Saints and the, "WAIT A MINUTE!" shouted the $20 dollar bill to the $1 dollar bill, WHAT'S A CHURCH?"

"One night the granddaughter came bouncing down the stairs dressed to go to a party wearing a see-through blouse with no bra. Her grandmother told her to go upstairs and dress decent. The young woman said "no, I want to show off my rosebuds" and went out the door. The next day the granddaughter came outside to find her grandmother wearing a see-through blouse without a bra. "What are you doing? My boyfriend and a couple of other friends are coming over any time now." She cried "Please go change your blouse, I am so embarrassed!" The older woman replied, "Well, if you can show off your rosebuds than I can show off my hanging baskets!"

Chapter 8

Excuses for Missing School

Being my mom was a teacher for many years, I am sure that is why I found some papers that listed some actual school excuse notes from parents, (with their original spelling), collected by schools all over the country. I will share some of them in hopes they will bring a smile or two. Heaven only knows that teachers can use some humor in their classrooms!

"Please excuse Roland from P.E. for a few days. He fell out of a tree and misplaced his hip."

"Carlos was absent yesterday because he was playing football. He was hurt in his growing part."

"Dear school: Please excuse John being absent on Jan 28, 29 30, 31 and 32.

"My son is under a doctor's care and should not take P.E. today. He had to be shot."

"Please excuse Gloria from Jim today. She is administrating."

"Morgan could not come to school today because she has been bothered by very close veins."

"*Please excuse Ray Friday from school. He has very loose vowels.*"

"*Irving was absent yesterday because he missed his bust.*"

"*Please excuse Bette, she has been sick and under the doctor.*"

"*Please excuse Jimmy from being. It was his father's fault.*"

"*I kept Billie home because she had to go Christmas shopping and I do not know her size.*"

"*Please excuse Jason from being absent yesterday. He had a cold and could not breed well.*"

"*Please excuse Mary from being absent yesterday. She was in bed with gramps.*"

"*Please excuse Pedro from school yesterday. He had (diahre) (dyrea) (direathe) the runs! The words in the parenthesis were crossed out. (My mom always believed you do have to give people credit for at least trying!)*"

"*Maryann was absent December 11-16, because she had a fever, sore throat, headache and upset stomach. Her sister was also sick with fever, sore throat. Her brother had a low-grade fever and ached all over. I wasn't the best either, sore throat and fever. There must be something going around, her father even got hot last night.*"

"*Please excuse little Timmy for not being in school yesterday. His father is gone and I could not get him ready as I was in bed with the doctor.*"

My mom loved kids so teaching kindergarten was a natural life choice for her teaching. She was noted for her innovative teaching skills. She had many humorous moments that she would share with us, but one of the funniest I remember I have to share with you. She always felt like you could keep a child's interest more by having them participate in what you were teaching. She taught in a Christian school so Bible stories were sometimes shared. On one particular day, she was telling the story of Daniel in the Lion's Den. Thinking that the kids would really enjoy playing the part of the lion, (and they did), she had them all on the floor crawling around and roaring like lions. Of course, she got on the floor with them to show them how to do it so they wouldn't be too loud or wild acting (we all know how that can be!) It just happened to be the day that the Superintendent of schools came to observe her kindergarten unannounced. He walked in the room along with the principal and there they all were crawling on the floor and roaring like lions including the teacher! She was somewhat embarrassed to have welcomed him this way but he actually got a kick out of this and saw that she really did take part with her kids! I don't think there would have been many kids that would have not loved being in her kindergarten class! In fact, some of them even kept in touch with her through the years.

Chapter 9

"That's When the Fight Started" Jokes

People knew my mom loved humor and they would sometimes send her some funny sayings or jokes. As I stated, I am not sure where these came from, or who created them, but they obviously liked humor too! Maybe we should all appreciate humor more. It could sure add some bright spots in people's lives when they may need it the most. There were some sayings titled, "That's when the Fight Started," that someone had sent her that I can remember her sharing with me. I will share a few of them with you. (A little slapstick humor.)

"One year a husband decided to buy his mother-in-law a cemetery plot as a Christmas gift. The next year he didn't buy her a gift and she asked him Why? He replied "Well. you still haven't used the gift I gave you last year!" That is when the fight started-----!

"My wife walked in the den and asked "What's on the TV?" I replied "lots of dust!" That is when the fight started----!"

"A woman was standing nude, looking in the bathroom mirror. She is not happy with what she sees, and says to her husband, "I feel horrible, I look fat, old and ugly. I really need you to pay me a

compliment." The husband replies, "Well, I can honestly say that your eyesight is darn near perfect!" That is when the fight started----!"

"I asked my wife "Where do you want to go for our anniversary?" It warmed my heart to see her face melt into sweet appreciation. "Somewhere we haven't been in a long time." "So, I suggested "How about the kitchen?" That is when the fight started----!

"My wife and I were watching "Who wants to be a Millionaire" while we were in bed. Feeling amorous I asked if she wanted to make love. "No" she answered. I then said "is that your final answer?" She didn't even look at me this time, simply saying "yes." So, I said, "then I like to phone a friend." That's when the fight started----!"

"I took my wife to a restaurant. The waiter, for some reason, took my order first. "I'll have the strip steak, medium rare, please." The waiter then asked," "aren't you worried about the mad cow?" "Nah," said the husband, "She can order for herself." That is when the fight started-------!"

Chapter 10

Meaning of Love from a Child's View

As I previously stated, my mom loved children and I always believed she was really a child at heart. I think that is why she related so well to them. She saved hundreds of things relating to children's education as well as humor. Many of her humorous children's stories have religious themes to them. She was a Sunday school teacher for many years as well as a Kindergarten teacher. She was a Christian herself and believed we needed to have and share humor with others. "Laughter is so good for the soul!" She, believed God has a sense of humor and looking at some of us here on earth, I believe she was right!

I found a prayer for children among her papers that I believe she prayed many times over her teaching years and I will share that with you.

"Let me lead a child Lord"

"How I want to lead a child to grasp your truths, Lord. A child on you to lean. Let me lead a child, Lord, their eyes can show such light; They seem so close to you, Lord, oh help me to lead them right. Let

me lead a child, Lord, there is no greater task. Let my heart be open to answer the truths of what they ask."

"We are always searching for the meaning of love. Each person has their own thoughts as to what it means to them. In a survey of four-to-eight-year-old children they gave answers we may never have thought of as adults. Even with their innocent and young minds, they have a deep grasp of that four-letter word." Here are some of their heart-warming definitions:

"Love is the first feeling you feel before all the bad stuff gets in the way." unknown

"When my grandmother got arthritis, she couldn't bend over and paint her toenails anymore, so my grandfather does it for her. His hands have arthritis too. That is love." Rebecca—age 8

"When someone loves you, the way they say your name is different. You know you name is safe in their mouth." Billy—age 4

"Love is when a girl puts on perfume and a boy puts on shaving lotion and they go out and smell each other." unknown

"Love is when you go out to eat and you give somebody most of your French fries without making them give you any of theirs." unknown

"Love is what makes you smile even when you're tired." Terri age 4

"Love is when my mommy makes coffee for my daddy and she takes a sip before giving it to him to make sure the taste is ok." Danny—age 7

"Love is when you kiss all the time. Then when you get tired of kissing, you still want to be together. My mommy and daddy are like that. They look gross when they kiss but they look happy and sometimes they kiss while dancing." Emily—age 8

"*Love is what is in the room with you at Christmas if you stop opening presents for a minute and look around.*" Bobby—age 7 (This is quite profound for adults let alone a child!)

"*If you want to learn to love better, you should start with a friend who hates you.*" Nikka---age 6 (Wow—we could all take that advice!

"*There are two kinds of love. Our love. God's love. But God makes both of them.*" unknown (That is pretty deep!)

"*Love is when you tell a guy you love his shirt, then he wears it every day.*" Noelle—age 7

"*My mommy loves me more than anybody. You don't see anyone else kissing me to sleep every night.*" unknown

"*Love is when mommy gives daddy the best piece of chicken.*" Elaine—age 5

"*Love is when mommy sees daddy smelly and sweaty and still says he is handsomer than Robert Redford.*" Chris—age 7

"*Love is when your puppy licks your face even after you have left him alone all day.*" unknown

"*You really shouldn't say "I love you" unless you mean it. But if you do mean it, you should say it a lot. People forget.*" Jessica---age 8

"*When you love someone, your eyelashes go up and down and little stars come out of you.*" Karen—age 7

"*Love make you sweat a lot.*" unknown

"*You never have to be lonely. There's always somebody to love even if it is just a squirrel or kitten.*" unknown

"You can break love, but it won't die." unknown

"When you are born and see your mommy's face for the first time. That's love." unknown

"God could have said magic words to make the nails fall off the cross, but he didn't. That is love." unknown (This has such insight and my favorite!)

"If you want somebody to love you, then just be yourself. Some people try to act like somebody else, somebody the boy likes better. I think the boy is not being very good if he does this to you and you should just find a nicer boy." Unknown

All I can say, is that I think we need to give kids a lot more credit for their understanding!

---

⁶⠀⌬⠀⁹

Chapter 11

Some Children's Humor

I came across a paper my mom had where a first-grade teacher had collected old and well-worn proverbs. She gave each child in her class the first half of the proverb, and they had to come up with the rest. Here are some of their answers. If you know the real saying it is even a bigger laugh!

"As you make your bed so shall you------mess it up!"

"Strike while the--------bug is close!"

"It is always darkest before-----Daylight Saving Time!"

"Never underestimate the power of --------Termites!"

"Don't bite the hand that--------Looks dirty!"

"A miss is as good as a --------Mr.!"

"There is none so blind as --------Helen Keller!"

"Two's company, three's--------The Musketeers!"

"If you lie down with dogs, you'll---------Stink in the morning!"

"Laugh and the whole world laughs with you, cry---------And you have to blow your nose!"

"A bird in the hand---------is going to poop!"

"Children should be seen and not--------Grounded or Spanked!"

"A penny saved is----------Not much!"

(You have got to love them. When you don't know the answer, at least you can be creative!)

Here are some more funny kid's sayings.

This is from a child's Science exam:

Q: How can you delay mile turning sour?

A: Keep it in the cow.

Q: Name the four seasons.

A: Salt, pepper, mustard, and vinegar.

Q: Name a major disease associated with cigarettes?

A: Premature death.

Q: What does "varicose" mean?

A: Nearby.

Q: What is the fibula?

A: A small lie.

Q: What happens to your body as you age?

A: When you get old, so do your bowels and you get intercontinental.

Q: Give the meaning of the term "Caesarean Section.""

A: The Caesarean Section is a district in Rome.

Q: What does the word benign mean?

A: Benign is what you will be after eight. (I love this one!)

Chapter 12

Kids Do Ask and Say the Darndest Things!

Here are some more children's stories that I thought you would enjoy and I know my mom would have love to share them with you.

"A seven-year-old told his teacher, "I don't want to scare you, but my daddy says that if I don't get better grades, somebody is going to get spanked!"

"I didn't know if my granddaughter had learned her colors yet, so I decided to test her. I would point to something and ask her what color it was. She would tell me, and she was always correct. But it was fun for me so I continued. At last, she headed for the door, saying "Grandma, I think you should try to figure some of these out for yourself!"

"My young grandson was visiting one day when he asked, "Grandma, do you know how you and God are alike?" I mentally polished my halo while I asked, "No dear, how are we alike?" "You're both old" he replied!"

"A Sunday school teacher asked, "Who can tell the story of Adam and Eve?" A child raised her hand and said, "First of all God created

Adam. Then he looked at Adam and thought, "I think I can do better. I'll try again. So, then he created Eve."

"A woman was trying hard to get the last of the ketchup out of the jar. Meanwhile the phone rang and she asked her 4-year-old daughter to answer the phone when she heard her say, "Mommy can't come to the phone to talk right now. She's hitting the bottle!"

"A little girl was spending the week-end with her grandmother. They decided to take a nature walk in the woods on Saturday morning. It had rained the night before and everything looked lush and beautiful. "It looks like an artist's painting here today," said her grandmother. I bet God painted this just for us!" "Yes," said the little girl "and he did it with his left hand." "A bit perplexed, the grandmother asked "What makes you say that?" "Well, we learned in Sunday school that Jesus sits on God's right hand!"

"One day a little girl was watching her mother do the dishes. She noticed that her mother had several strands of white hair sticking out in contrast to her brunette color hair. She looks at her mom and inquisitively asks, "Why are some of your hairs white, Mom?" "Well," said her mom, every time that you do something wrong and make me cry or unhappy, one of my hairs turns white." The little girl thought about this revelation and then said. "So, mama, how come ALL of grandma's hairs are white?"

"A little boy couldn't wait to tell his father about the movie he had just watched on television, "20,000 Leagues Under the Sea." The scenes with the submarine and the giant octopus had kept him wide-eyed." "In the middle of telling the story, his father interrupted his son. "What caused the submarine to sink, son?" "Dad," he replied, it was the 20,000 leaks!"

"A little boy got lost at the YMCA and found himself in the women's locker room. When he was spotted, the room burst into shrieks with *ladies grabbing towels and running for cover. The little boy watched in amazement and then asked, "What's the matter, haven't you ever seen a little boy before?"*

"I was driving with my three young children one warm summer evening when a woman in the convertible ahead of us stood up and waved. She was stark naked! As I was reeling from the shock, I heard my five-year-old shout from the back seat, "Mom, that lady isn't wearing a seat belt!"

"One summer evening during a violent thunderstorm a mother was tucking her small boy into bed. She was about to turn off the light when he asked her with a tremor in his voice, "Mommy, will you sleep with me tonight?" The mother smiled and gave him a reassuring hug. "I can't dear," she said, "I have to sleep in daddy's room." A long silence was broken at last by his shaky little voice, "The big sissy!"

"A Sunday school teacher asked just before she dismissed the class to go to church, "Why is it necessary to be quiet in church?" Little Johnny jumped up and yelled, "Because people are sleeping!"

"While walking along the sidewalk in front of the church, our minister heard the intoning of a prayer that made his collar wilt. Apparently, his five-year-old son and his playmates had found a dead Robin. Feeling a proper burial should be performed, they had secured a small box, and cotton batting, then dug a hole and made ready for the disposal of the deceased. The minister's son was chosen to say the appropriate prayers and with sonorous dignity intoned his version of what he thought his father always said: "Glory be unto the faaather, and unto the sonnnn, and into the hole he goooes!" (I want this line used at my funeral!)

"A little boy opened the big Family Bible. He was fascinated as he fingered through the old pages. Suddenly, something fell out of the Bible. He picked it up and looked at it. What he saw was an old

leaf that had been pressed between the pages. "Mama, look what I have found," the boy called out. "What have you got there, dear?" With astonishment in the young boy's voice, he answered, "I think it's Adam's underwear!"

"A Sunday school was studying the Ten Commandments. They were ready to discuss the last one. The teacher asked if anyone could tell her what it was. Susie raised her hand, stood tall, and quoted, "Thou shalt not take the covers off thy neighbor's wife." Clarence A. Wildeboer

---
⌒⌒⌒

Chapter 13

Learning From a Child

Some of the stories I found among my mom's papers had heart-warming themes. Young children have such an innocence that come through their thoughts and actions. So pure and honest. We could all take a few lessons from them! Here are a few that warmed my heart! I hope they will yours too.

"A four-year old's elderly neighbor had recently lost his wife. Upon seeing the man crying, the little boy went into the old man's yard, climbed into his lap and just sat there. When he came home, his mother asked him what he had said to the neighbor. The little boy replied, "nothing, mom, I just helped him cry."

"A six-year-old was overheard saying the Lord's Prayer at a church service: And forgive us our trash passes as we forgive those who passed trash against us! (I'm sure this was one of my mom's favorites!)

"After church services seven-year-old Brian said to the preacher, "When I grow-up I am going to give you some money." "Well, thank you Brian," replied the preacher, but why are you thinking of doing that?" "Because my daddy said you are the poorest preacher we have ever had."

"A mother invited some people over for dinner. At the table, she turned to their six-year-old daughter and said, "Would you like to say the blessing?" "I really don't know what to say," replied the girl shyly. "Just say what you heard mommy say," relied the mother. The daughter bowed her head and said, "Lord, why on earth did I invite all these people to dinner?

"A Kindergarten teacher was observing her classroom of children while they were drawing. She would occasionally walk around to see each child's work. As she got to one little girl who was working diligently, she asked what the drawing was. The little girl replied, "I'm drawing God." The teacher paused and said, "But no one knows what God looks like." Without missing a beat, or looking up from her drawing, the girl replied, "They will in a minute."

"While working for an organization that delivers lunches to elderly shut-ins, I use to take my five-year-old daughter on my afternoon rounds. She was intrigued by the various appliances of old age, especially the canes, walkers, and wheel chairs. One day I found her staring at a pair of false teeth soaking in a dish. As I braced for the inevitable barrage of questions, she merely turned and whispered, "The tooth fairy will never believe this!"

"A teacher in a first-grade classroom was discussing a picture of a family. One of the little boys in the picture had a different color hair than the other family members. One child suggested that maybe he was adopted. "I know about adoption, said one of the little girls, because my mommy and daddy adopted me." What is adoption several children asked her? "It's when you grow in your mommy's heart instead of her tummy!"

"A Kindergarten student was trying out for a part in a school play. His mother had told her good friend that he had his heart set on being in it, though she feared he wouldn't be chosen. On the day the parts were awarded, her friend went with her to pick him up

after school. Jamie rushed up to his mom, his eyes shining with pride and excitement. "Guess what mom," he shouted, and then said those words that will remain a lesson to me. "I've been chosen to clap and cheer!"

I thought about that one. I thought it was really a clever way to include all the kids in the play and then it hit me how important that part really was! We need cheerleaders in our lives. Did you have a cheerleader in your life that cheered you on to do something you never thought you could? That one person can change our lives. We can be a cheerleader in someone's life and that could even change that person's life! My mom was an encourager (pretty much the same as a cheerleader to me) so I understood at a young age how important that was. It is so easy to forget how meaningful and important some caring actions and words are. It can especially build that so important trait of self-esteem in our children. Thank you, mom for your encouragement!

Chapter 14

Children Talk of Angels and God

My mom loved angels and had a large collection of them. When you couldn't think of a gift for her, there were always the angels. When she learned that, according to the Bible, there was no mention of female angels, that was rather disappointing to her. The ones mentioned were always men. She still loved her all-female collection! I could never remember seeing a figure of a male angel. I think it could be a future business for someone! Speaking of angels, I found a paper in her children's collection of material that asked younger children what they thought of angels. Here are some of their answers.

"Everyone's got it wrong. Angels don't wear halos anymore. I forget why, but scientists are working on it." Greg—age 6

"My guardian angel helps me with my math but he isn't much good with science." Henry—age 7

"I only know of two angels, Hark and Harold." Tommy—age 5

"Angels don't drink but they eat holy cows." Kate—age 6

"Angels talk all the way while they are flying up to heaven. The main subject is about where you went wrong before you got dead." Dan---age 8

"Angels work for God and watch over kids when he has to do something else." Sherry—age 6

"Angels have a lot to do and keep very busy. If, you lose a tooth, an angel comes through your window and leaves money under your pillow. When it gets cold, angels go South for the winter." Sara-age 6

"Angels live in cloud houses made by God and his Son, who is a very good carpenter." Jared—age 7

"Angels are girls because they have to wear dresses and boys don't go for that." Antonio—age 8

(He hasn't learned about the "only male" theory yet!)

And my favorite:

"What I don't get about angels is why, when someone is in love, they shoot arrows at them!"

I also came across some children's letters to God that I wanted to share. I am sure you'll have a few smiles added to your day.

"Dear God, I went to this wedding and they kissed right in church. "Is that ok?"

"Dear God, what does it mean You are a jealous God? I thought you had everything."

"Dear God, thank you for my baby brother, but what I prayed for was a puppy."

"Dear God, it rained for our whole vacation and is my father mad! He said some things about You that people are not supposed to say, but I hope You will not hurt him anyway, your friend (but I am not going to tell you who I am!)"

"Dear God, why is Sunday school on Sunday? I thought it was supposed to be our day of rest?"

"Dear God, maybe Cain and Abel would not kill each other so much if they had their own rooms. It works with my brother."

"Dear God, please send me a pony. I have never asked for anything before. You can look that up."

"Dear God, I bet it is hard for You to love all of everybody in the whole world. There are only four people in our family and I can never do it."

"Dear God, if you watch me in church Sunday, I'll show you my new shoes."

"Dear God, we read in school that Thomas Edison made light. But in Sunday school they said you did. So, I bet he stole your idea!"

Here are a few more quotes about children that I thought were quite humorous:

"You can fool some of the people all the time and all the people some of the time, but you can never fool mom!" Unknown

"Children: you spend the first two years of their life teaching them to walk and talk. Then you spend the next sixteen telling them to sit down and shut up!" Phyllis Diller

"Grandchildren are God's reward for not killing your children!" Tony Campolo

"Cleaning your house while your kids are still growing, is like clearing the driveway before it stops snowing!" Phyllis Diller

"There is only one pretty child in the world and every mother has it!" Chinese Proverb

"Children are natural mimics, who act like their parents despite every effort to teach them good manners!" Mark Twain

"Mothers of teens know why animals eat their young!" Unknown

Here are a few truths about life that children learn:

"No matter how hard you try, you can't Baptize cats!" Laura--- age 13

"When your mom is mad at your dad, don't let her brush your hair!" Morgan-- age11

"If your sister hits you, don't hit her back. They always catch the second person!" Michael—age10

"Never ask your three-year-old brother to hold a tomato!" Unknown

"My mama told me that sometimes people have to cry out their tears to make room for a heart full of smiles!" Unknown

"You can't trust dogs to watch your food!" St. Patrick

"Don't sneeze when someone is cutting your hair!" Unknown

"You can't hide a piece of broccoli in a glass of milk!" H. Jackson Brown Jr.

"The best place to be when you are sad is in Grandma's lap." Unknown

Before I close out the children's section, I will share several final stories that I feel are ones my mom really liked.

> "After church on Sunday, A young boy suddenly announced to his mother, "Mom I have decided to be a minister when I grow up." "That is fine son, but what made you decide that?" "Well, I have to go to church on Sunday anyway, and I figure it will be more fun to stand up and yell than to sit and listen!"

This is a gem:

> "One morning near Easter time, a little boy went to his Grandparents house with two of his friends to visit. The grandfather thought it would be a great opportunity to tell the boys the true meaning of this Christian holiday. He asked the boys "What do we do at Easter?" One of the friends quickly answered "Oh my family gets together and we eat a lot of food like turkey, cranberry sauce and pumpkin pie." "No replied the grandfather, that is Thanksgiving." The other friend answered, "Oh, that's when everyone comes over and we open a lot of presents and sing songs."" "No, that's Christmas." The grandfather was anxious to hear his grandson's response to his question, and thought surely, he would know the purpose and true meaning of Easter. His grandson said "I know, Easter is when we celebrate the resurrection of Jesus Christ, our Lord and Savior." The grandfather was very proud of the boy's answer and smiled, but the boy continued, "and every Spring, when Jesus comes out of the grave, if he sees His shadow, we'll have six more weeks of Winter!"

All parents can relate to this following one and it is one of our worst nightmares.

> "A father passing by his son's bedroom was astonished to see that his bed was nicely made and everything was picked up. Then he saw an envelope propped up on the pillow that was addressed to "dad.' With the worst premonition he opened the envelope with trembling hands

and read the letter. *Dear Dad, it is with great regret and sorrow that I am writing to you. I had to elope with my new girlfriend because I wanted to avoid a scene with you and mom. I have been finding real passion with Stacy and she is so nice, but I knew you would not approve of all her piercings, and tattoos, or her tight motorcycle clothes and the fact she is much older than I am. But it is not only passion dad, she is pregnant. Stacy said that we would be happy. She owns a trailer in the woods and has a stack of firewood that will last us all Winter. We share a dream of having more children. Stacy has opened my eyes to the fact that marijuana really doesn't hurt anyone. We will be growing it for ourselves and trading it with other people the live nearby for cocaine and ecstasy. In the meantime, we will pray that science will find a cure for AIDS so Stacy can get better. She deserves it. Don't worry dad, I'm 15 and know how to take care of myself. Someday I'm sure that we will be back to visit so that you can get to know your grandchildren. Love, John*

P.S. Dad, none of this is true. I'm over at Tommy's house. I just wanted to remind you that there are worse things in life than the report card that is in my center drawer. I love you. Call me when it is safe to come home!"

Chapter 15

Some Getting Older Humor

Some of the funniest jokes and stories that I found were about getting older. Maybe it brings more smiles when we can identify with the sayings. I know my mom surely did and I find myself laughing more at them. I think that tells me something! How about you? I would like to start with a poem that I found with the author unknown.

"Just a line to say I'm living. That I am not among the dead. Though I'm getting more forgetful and all mixed up in the head. I got use to my arthritis and to my dentures I'm resigned. I can manage my bifocals but God I miss my mind! For sometimes I can't remember when I stand at the foot of the stairs, if I must go up for something, or have I just come down from there? And before the fridge so often my poor mind is filled with doubt, have I just put food away or have I come to take some out? And there's a time when it is dark, I stop and shake my head, I don't know if I'm retiring or if I'm getting out of bed? So, if it is my turn to write to you there's no need getting sore, I may think I have written and don't want to be a bore. So, remember that I love you and wish that you were near, but now it's nearly mail time so I must say "good bye dear." Here I stand before the mail box with a face so very red, instead of mailing you my letter, I went and opened it instead!"

(If you are in a club or group of more mature people, bring this along to read. People will love it.)

In continuing, here are some humorous quotes about getting older that I found.

"Maybe it is true that life begins at fifty. But everything else starts to fall out or spread out!" Phyllis Diller

"You're getting older when you don't care where your spouse goes, as long as you don't have to go along!" Unknown

"Getting old is like climbing a mountain; you get a little out of breath but the view is much better!' Ingrid Bergman

"Middle age is when work is a lot less fun, and fun a lot more work!" Laurence J. Peters

"Statistics show that at the age of seventy, there are five women to every man. Isn't that the darndest time for a guy to get those odds!" Unknown

"By the time a man is wise enough to watch his step, he is too old to go anywhere!" Billy Crystal

"A man has reached middle age when he is cautioned to slow down by the doctor instead of the police!" Joan Rivers

"You know you are getting older when the girls at the office start confiding in you!" Unknown

"At my age, "getting a little action" means I don't have to take a laxative." Unknown

"The aging process could be slowed down if it has to work its way through Congress!" Will Rodgers

"You know you're into middle age when you realize that caution is the only thing you care to exercise!" Unknown

"You're getting older when getting lucky means you find your car in the parking lot!" Unknown

"You're getting older when you are sitting in a rocker and can't get it started!" Unknown

"Last will and testament of a senior to his children: Being of sound mind, I have spent all my money!" Unknown

"A cardiologist's diet to help you live longer: Ready? If it tastes good, Spit it out!" Unknown

"Reminder: age is all in your mind. The trick is to keep from creeping down into your body!" Anonymous

"You sink your teeth into a steak and they stay there!" Unknown

"My wild oats have turned into prunes and all-bran!" Unknown

"Your knees buckle but your belt won't!" Unknown

"You finally get your head together and your body starts falling apart!" Caryn Leschen

"Everything hurts and what doesn't hurt doesn't work!" Hy Gardner

"My mind not only wanders, it sometimes leaves completely!" Daniel Tosh

"I still have a full deck I just shuffle slower now!" Unknown

"Your birthday reminds me of my old school mate—Yung No-Mo!" Unknown

"The older you get, the tougher it is to lose weight, because by then your body and your fat are really good friends!" Bob Hope

"Old is when going bra-less pulls all the wrinkles out of your face!" Unknown

"Old is when your friends compliment your new alligator shoes when you are actually barefoot!" Phyllis Diller

"Old is when an "all-nighter" means not getting up to use the bathroom!" Unknown

"Finally, after all these years, I discovered what Victoria's Secret is. The secret is that no one over 30 can fit into their stuff!" Unknown

"Old is when your sweetie says "Let's go upstairs and make love" and you answer "Pick one, I can't do both!" Unknown

Research has shown that people who stay positive about getting older, live on the average at least seven and a half years longer. My mom surpassed that length, I am sure. She believed that the more positivity, humor, fun, compassion, (among some of the traits she had), the more happiness you will find in your life. Actually, getting older is a part of life we all will encounter if we live long enough. Understanding that fact, and embracing the wisdom we have learned through the years, we can make it some of the best and most productive years of our lives. Today, society is so youth conscious that is difficult to embrace that concept. We need to instill in our children that youth is fleeting. We need to enjoy that time but also look forward to sharing the wisdom and knowledge we have learned through the years hoping that can help others live more positive and productive lives.

Chapter 16

More Humorous Stories for the Young at Heart

I have to share some more humorous stories about older folks that were among my mom's papers, as they will make your day, and my mom would have loved that!

Retirement from a child's eyes!

"After a Christmas break, a teacher asked her young pupils to write a story about how they spent their holidays. One small boy wrote the following: "We always use to spend Christmas with Grandma and Grampa. They use to live here in a big brick home, but Grandpa got retarded and they moved to Florida. Now they live in a place with a lot of other retarded people. They all live in little tin boxes. They ride on big three-wheeled tricycles and they all wear name tags as they don't know who they are! They go to a big building they call a wrecked hall, but they must have got it fixed because it is all right now. They play games and do exercises but they don't do them very good. There is a swimming pool there. They go into it and just stand there with their hats on. I guess they don't know how to swim. As you go into the park, there is a doll house with a little man sitting in it. He watches all day so they can't get out without him seeing them. When they sneak-out they go to the beach and pick up shells. My Grandma use to bake cookies and stuff, but I guess she forgot how. Nobody cooks,

they just eat out. They eat the same thing every night, early birds. Some of the people are so retarded they don't know how to cook at all so my grandma, and grandpa, bring food into the wrecked hall and they call it "pot luck." My Grandpa says he worked all his life and earned his retardment. I wish they would move back up here, but I guess the little man in the doll house won't let them out!"

"Two old gentlemen were sitting on a bench under a big Oak tree. One of the gentlemen said, I'm 83 years old and am full of aches and pains. I know you are about my age. How do you feel?" "Oh, he said, I "feel just like a new born babe." "Really like a new born babe asked the first gentlemen? "Yep," he replied, no hair, no teeth and I just think I wet my pants!"

"I have had two bypasses, Prostrate cancer, Diabetes, I am half blind, can't hear anything less than a jet plane, take 40 different medicines that make me dizzy, woozie, and I am subject to blackouts. I have bouts of dementia, have poor circulation, hardly feel my hands and feet anymore. I can't remember if I'm 82 or 92 and have lost all my friends, but thank God I can still drive!"

I am sure I have driven on the road with this guy. You may have too!

"Three old guys were out walking. The first one said, "Windy, isn't it?" "No, it's Thursday said the second guy." "I'm thirsty too, so let's go have a drink," said the third!"

"An elderly Gentlemen had serious hearing trouble for years. But he had found a doctor who had found and fixed the problem. When he went back for a check-up the doctor said to him, "With your hearing so perfect now, I bet your family is really pleased!" "Well," the man said, "I haven't told them yet. I just listen to their conversations and I have changed my Will three times!"

"*Two elderly people lived in an assisted living center. He was a widower and she was a widow and they had known each other for a number of years before coming to live here after their spouses had died. One evening there was a community supper in the clubhouse. The two were at the same table, across from one another. As the meal went on, he took a few admiring glances at her and finally gathered the courage to ask her, "Will you marry me?" After the six seconds of "careful consideration," she answered "Yes, yes, I will!" The meal ended, with a few more pleasant exchanges, they went to their respective places. The next morning, he was troubled. "Did she say "yes" or did she say "no?" He could not recall! Not even a faint memory. With trepidation, he went to the phone and called her. First, he explained he didn't remember as well as he used to. Then he reviewed the lovely evening past. As he gained a little more courage, he inquired, "When I asked you to marry me, did you say "yes" or did you say "no?" He was delighted to hear her say, "Why I said Yes, yes I will and I meant it with all my heart." "I am so glad you called though, because I couldn't remember who had asked me!"*

"*An elderly woman was thinking to herself. Everything is farther away than it used to be. It is even twice as far to the corner and they have added a hill! I have given up running for the bus; it leaves earlier than it used to. It seems to me they are even making stairs steeper than in the old days. And I have noticed the smaller print they use in the newspapers now. There is no sense in asking anyone to read aloud anymore, as everybody speaks in such a low voice, I can hardly hear them. The material in dresses is so skimpy now, especially around the hips and waist, that is almost impossible to reach one's shoelaces. And the sizes don't run the way they use to. The 12's and 14's are so much smaller. Even the people are changing. They are so much younger that they use to be when I was their age. On the other hand, people my age look so much older than I do. I ran into an old classmate the other day and she has aged so much that she didn't recognize me. I got to thinking about the poor dear while I was combing my hair this* morning and in doing so, I glanced at my own reflection. Really now, they don't even make good mirrors like they use to!"

"Remember, old folks are worth a fortune, with silver in their hair, gold in their teeth, stones in their kidneys, lead in their feet and gas in their stomachs!" Unknown

"I have become a little older since I saw you last and a few changes have come into my life. Frankly, I have become a frivolous old gal. I am seeing four gentlemen every day. As soon as I wake up, Will Power does help me get out of bed. Then I go see John. His demands are rather draining. Then Charlie Horse comes along and he takes a lot of my time and attention. When he leaves, Arthur Ritis shows up and stays the rest of the day. He doesn't like to stay in one place, so he takes me from joint to joint. After such a busy day I am really tired and glad to go to bed with Ben Gay. What a life!"

"P.S. The preacher came to call the other day. He said at my age I should start thinking about the hereafter. I told him, oh, I do that all the time. No matter where I am, in the parlor, upstairs, in the kitchen or down in the basement, I am constantly thinking, what am I hereafter?"

Chapter 17

Funny Newspaper Ads

We probably all have seen an ad or two in a newspaper, magazine, or on the wall that didn't read as it was meant to due to spelling errors, punctuation, or improper wording. I found some humorous ones among my mom's papers that were said to be posted in newspapers.

"A superb inexpensive restaurant. Fine food expertly served by waitresses in appetizing forms.".

"Now is your chance to get your ears pierced and get an extra pair to take home too!"

"Tired of cleaning yourself? Let me do it!"

"For Sale—eight puppies from a German Shepard and an Alaskan Hussy."

"Wanted: A man to take care of a horse that does not drink or smoke."

"Our bikinis are exciting. They are simply the tops!"

"Three-year-old teacher needed for pre-school. Experience preferred,"

"*Experienced mom will care for your child. Fenced yard. Meals and Smacks included.*"

"*Auto Repair Service: Free pick-up and delivery. Try us once and you'll never go anywhere again.*"

"*Dog For Sale: Eats anything and is especially fond of children.*"

"*Repair man, honest. Will take anything.*"

"*For Rent: Six room hated apartment.*"

"*Stock up and save. Limit: one*"

Here are some signs that were seen on businesses—too funny!

"*Sign in a laundromat: Please remove all your clothes when the light goes out.*"

"*Sign in an office breakroom: After the coffee breaks, the staff should empty the coffee pot and stand upside down on the draining board.*"

"*Sign on an electrician's truck: Let us remove your shorts.*"

"*Outside a muffler shops window: No appointment necessary. We hear you coming.*"

"*In an Optometrist's office: If you don't see what you're looking for, you've come to the right place.*" (*One of my favorites!*)

"*Butcher's window: Let me meet your needs.*"

"*Sign on a computer store door: Out for a quick byte.*"

"*Sign seen posted in a conference center: For anyone that has children and doesn't know it, there is a day care on the first floor.*"

"On a repair shop door: We can repair anything! (Please knock hard on door. The bell doesn't work.")

"On a restroom wall: Toilet out of order. Please use the floor below."

"Notice in a farmer's field: The farmer allows walkers to cross the field for free but the bull charges." (I would say that this farmer has a great sense of humor!)

"Sign outside a secondhand store: We exchange anything---Bicycles, washing machines, and etc. Why not bring your wife along and get a wonderful bargain!"

I found a few more signs seen outside churches that made me smile.

"Come in and pray today. Beat the Christmas rush!"

"Try our Sundays. They are better that Baskin Robbins!"

"Sign broken. Message inside this Sunday!"

"Free trip to heaven. Details inside!"

"How will you spend eternity—Smoking or Non-smoking!"

"No God—No Peace. Know God—Know Peace!"

(Great marketing strategy as humor appeals to all of us.)

Chapter 18

Humorous Newspaper Headlines

Again, wrong punctuation or putting wrong placement of words, makes these newspaper ads humorous. They were found in real newspaper headlines.

"Police Begin Campaign to Run down Jaywalkers."

"Farmer Bill Dies in House."

"Policeman helps Dog Bite Victim."

"Kids make Nutritious Snacks."

"City Residents Can Drop off Trees."

"Include Your Children When Baking Cookies."

"Red Tape Holds Up New Bridge."

"Air Head Fired."

"New Study of Obesity Looks for Larger Test Group."

"Hospital is Sued BY 7foot doctors."

"Stud Tires Out."

"If Strike isn't settled Quickly, It May Last Awhile."

"Eye Drops Off Shelf."

"Safety Experts Say School Bus Passengers Should be Belted."

"Two Sisters Reunited After 18 Years in Checkout Counter."

"Chef Throws his Heart into Feeding the Needy."

"Juvenile Court to Try Shooting Defendant."

"Astronaut Takes Blame for Gas in Spacecraft."

"Some Pieces of Rock Hudson Sold at Auction."

"Panda Mating Fails; Veterinarian Takes Over."

"Local High School Drop Outs Cut in Half."

"Teacher Strikes Idle Kids."

"Iraq Head Seeks Arms."

"Wedding Dress for sale. Worn Once by Mistake!"

"Miners Refuse to Work After Death."

"I think we can all agree that words, and how we say them, make all the difference on how our statements come across. My mom had a little paper that said: Before you speak, think. If you have seen this before it is always good to be reminded. I personally have to "THINK" about this quite often! Maybe it will help you too!"

T------is it True?

H-----is it Helpful?

I------is it Inspiring?

N-----is it Necessary?

K-----is it Kind?

Wow, that is a lot to THINK about before speaking—maybe I will just try to speak slower or sometimes maybe not at all!

Chapter 19

Being a Good Hostess

My mom was a really good hostess. She always wanted everyone to feel they were a part of her gatherings. If she was giving a special dinner, you would usually have a creative name tag at your place at the table and a joke or riddle under your dinner plate. When the time came for some entertainment, each person would read their joke or ask their riddle. This always brought laughter and started conversations that all could be involved in. If you have never done this, I suggest you try it at your next gathering. It can really break the ice. My mom also loved playing games. She would have everyone play them or take partners. Even the most reserved or quiet people tend to be competitive when challenged. She usually had a little gift that the winner would receive. I will give you some examples of riddles she used.

"By night they come out without being fetched, by day they are lost without being stolen. What are they?"

Answer---(Stars!)

"What do you get if you if you cross an alley cat with a canary?"

Answer—-(Peeping Tom!)

"What do you call a grocery clerk in China?"

Answer----(Chinese Checker!)

"What is an honest opinion openly expressed?"

Answer----(A Yawn!)

"What are the only creatures you eat before they are born and after they are dead?"

Answer----(Chickens!)

"What day do chickens hate the most?"

Answer----(Friday's!)

"Why did the tomato turn red?"

Answer----(He saw the salad dressing!)

"What do you get when you cross a rabbit with a termite?"

Answer----(Bugs Bunny!)

"If you drop a hat in the Red Sea, what does it become?"

Answer----(It becomes wet as the Red Sea s not really red!)

"What can you hold without ever touching it."

Answer----(Your breath!)

"What do you get when you cross an elephant with a fish?"

Answer (Swimming trunks!)

You can ask factual riddles like these examples:

'What state has the highest percentage of people who walk to work?"

Answer----(Alaska)

"What was the original color of Coca-Cola?"

Answer----(Green)

"What day of the year has more collect calls that any others?"

Answer---(Father's Day.) Most people think it is Mother's Day.

"What do bullet proof vests, fire escapes, windshield wipers, and laser printers all have in common?"

Answer----(All invented by women!)

"If you were to spell out numbers, how far would you have to go to find the letter "A?"

Answer----(One thousand!) I will just believe that!

"Question: I can be created by humans, but they cannot control me. I suck on wood, plastic, paper, and flesh alike. I can be more of a hindrance than help at times. What am I?"

Answer----(A baby!)

"Question: I have many feathers to help me fly. I have a body and head, but I am not alive. It is your strength that determines how far I go. You can hold me in your hand but I am never thrown. What am I?"

Answer--- (An arrow!)

"Question: There are 20 people in an empty square room. Each person has full sight of the entire room, and everyone in it, without turning your head or body or moving in any way (other than eyes.) Where can you place an apple so that all but one person can see it?"

Answer----(Place the apple on one person's head!)

"Question: You are walking through a field and you find something to eat. It doesn't have bones, and it doesn't have meat. You pick it up and put it in your pocket. You take it home and put it on a shelf, but 3 days later it walks away. What is it?"

(It's an egg!)

"Question: A murderer is sentenced to death. He has to choose between 3 rooms for his sentence. The first is full of a raging fire. The second is full of assassins with loaded guns and the third is full of lions that haven't eaten in 3 years. What is the safest room for him?"

(If he were a smart murderer, he'd pick room 3. If those lions hadn't eaten in 3 years, I am sure they would be dead!

"A woman shoots her husband. After she hold him under water for over 3 minutes, and then she hangs him. After some time, they both go out together. How is that possible?"

(The woman is a photographer. She shot a picture of her husband, put it in developer and then hung it out to dry!) I bet you didn't see that coming!

I am sure you have some of your own jokes, riddles or stories to share. Just keep it simple and humorous. Remember, this is to have fun!

Chapter 20

A Little More Humor

As I previously mentioned, my mom was a Christian and she taught us 3 girls what that meant. She had many inspirational books and material to share on this subject. Because it was such a big part of her life, I want to share some of this material with you. I'll start with a prayer she loved and had for a long time. It supposedly was a prayer that was posted in St. Peter's Church, in Bermuda. Though written in a somewhat humorous way, she really hoped she could learn to do these things. I can honestly say she mostly succeeded!

"Lord, thou know better than I know myself, that I am growing older and will someday be old. (My mom really succeeded here!) Keep me from being too talkative, (that is debatable), and from the particularly fatal habit of thinking I must say something on every subject and on every occasion. Release me from craving to straighten out everybody's affairs. Keep my mind free from the recital of endless details. Give me wings to get to the point. I ask for Grace enough to listen to the tales of other's pain. Help me to endure them with patience. Seal my lips on my own aches and pains—they are increasing and my love of rehearsing them is becoming stronger as the years go by. Teach me the glory lesson occasionally, that I may be mistaken. (That was a work in progress for my mom!) Keep me reasonably sweet. I do not

want to be a saint as some of them are hard to live with, but a sour old woman is one of the crowning works of the devil. (Mom passed that with flying colors!) Make me thoughtful but not moody, helpful but not bossy. With my vast store of wisdom, it seems a pity not to use it all—but thy know, Lord, that I want a few friends at the end!" (*That she had!*)

Got to love the humor! I am sure Mom did!

My mom really appreciated life. She liked learning new things and making new friends. She did not hear well, and that was somewhat of a challenge, but we finally talked her into going to a hearing specialist and she reluctantly agreed. According to her, people just needed to speak up and clearer! I took her to a hearing specialist who tested her hearing. I think he really was surprised that she never had worn hearing aids. After letting her hear what voices sound like while wearing them, I believe that really showed her how much better she could hear and that having a pair might be the best. Breathing a sigh of relief, I felt we could have much nicer conversations without the repetitiveness of words. She had them about 6 months with some complaints, like they made her ears itch or she had to charge them too often, but they did improve her hearing. One evening she came into my computer room to ask me something and we talked for a while and then her hearing aids started ringing which happens when the charge gets low. She had worn them most of the day so the ringing wasn't unusual. She proceeded to take them out and hold them in her hand along with a kleenex she had been holding. We talked awhile longer and then she left to retire for the evening. About ten minutes later she came out and said she thought she had done something serious. She could not find her hearing aids and was afraid she had thrown them in the toilet along with the Kleenex! It was too late to see if we could fish them out as she had already flushed it down! I felt sick as I knew she had paid several thousand dollars for them.

But my mom, although she felt badly about it, just decided there was nothing she could do about it and life goes on! She had a unique ability not to let the past weigh her down with things she couldn't change. She felt you just needed to get on with life! I wish I could do that, but I never got that ability from her either, and this too, I am still trying to accomplish! Yes, to her, life moved on quickly and we need to work on things we can do now and not put them off until tomorrow. Don't wait to call your friends, invite people you enjoy over, tell someone how much they mean to you, smile at someone daily, and keep a heart and mind that's willing. Sometime soon may be too late. She would encourage you to do it now and make each day worthwhile!

Chapter 21

Some Good Questions and Answers to Remember

Among her papers I found a group of sentences and what some people thought were the best answers to them. I found this quite inspiring and hope you will also.

"The greatest shot in the arm--Encouragement."

"The greatest problem to overcome---Fear."

"The most effective sleeping pill---Peace of Mind."

"The most crippling disease---Excuses."

"The surest way to limit God—Unbelief."

"The most powerful force in life---Love."

"The most dangerous piranha—A Gossiper."

"The greatest life-giver---The Creator."

"The world's most incredible computer—The Brain."

"The worst thing to be without---Hope

"The deadliest weapon—The Tongue."

"The two most power-filled words--"I Can."

"The greatest asset--Faith."

"The most worthless emotion—Self Pity."

"The most beautiful attire—A Smile."

"The most prized possession---Self Esteem."

"The most powerful channel of communication---Prayer."

"The most contagious spirit—Enthusiasm."

"The most urgent need---Salvation."

"The GREATEST—God."

I believe that most of us can take a lesson from the above paper as I am sure my mom did. I know it was really good for me to think about and I hope it was for you too. I am sure that most of us do not realize what impact our words, actions and attitudes have on others. Just a kind word, a smile or even an unexpected helping hand can uplift someone's day. Maybe they will even pass it on!

I also found a poem that my mom had cut out from somewhere and she had written a few words on it. I thought it worth sharing. It is titled "An Old Oak Tree."

"In times of trial my Grammy said she was like an old Oak tree: Weathered and worn through trial and storm, not easily moved from its place. Branches are lost, in tempest tossed, thrown done by a

buffeting storm. But as morning breaks what remains is what's best. God's pruning, we would say. The branches she lost were at great cost and too many to count, I'm afraid. I once prayed a prayer that I could be just like her that old Oak tree. Oh, how I wish I had not! It's not easy to be strong or fun to be old and weathered. Yet my hope is that just like Grammy and the old Oak tree, I'll be beautiful, useful, and inspiring to those that come after me."

After the last sentence, my mom had written that "this is my prayer too!" I can say mom, that you have been truly inspiring to many, children and adults as well. Yes mom, I would say that your prayer was answered!

Chapter 22

Some Things I Have Learned In My Life

I also came across some papers that she had save that told of "things I have learned in my life." We all learn things as we move along in life. Some we are glad to learn and others we wish we hadn't learned at all. We also wish that we had learned some sooner! My mom, obviously living on this earth for 103 years, had learned her share of many things. I will list some that were on her papers.

> "I have learned many things from my life. I promise you not a sermon but would like to pass on some of the things I have learned."

> "I have learned that without God, life would have no meaning."

> "I have learned that a smile instead of a frown works wonders."

> "I have learned that by keeping your sunny side up everything turns out better."

> "I have found out that being thankful for what we have, instead of complaining about what we don't have, is the way to go."

> "I have found out that laughter eases tension—laugh until it works!"

"I have learned that doing kind deeds for others makes you really happy."

"I have learned that you shouldn't go through life with a catcher's mitt on both hands. You need to be able to throw something back."

"On the real bad days when everything hurts and what doesn't hurt doesn't work, get out your Bible. You will find help."

"I have learned that even when I have pains, I don't have to be one."

"I have learned that everyone can use prayer."

"I have learned that if you pursue happiness, it will elude you-but if you focus on your family, the needs of others, and doing the very best you can, happiness will find you."

"I have learned that it pays to believe in miracles, and to tell you the truth, I have seen several."

"I have learned that making a living is not the same as making a life."

"I've learned that if you want to cheer yourself up, you should try cheering someone else up."

"I've learned that every day you should reach out and touch someone. People love the human touch—holding hands, a warm hug, or just a friendly touch on the back."

"I've learned that I still have a lot to learn!"

It is said that you should learn at least one new thing every day. That is a goal all of us should try to reach. Even at 103 years of age, I can say that my mom reached that goal.

Chapter 23

In Conclusion

Maybe we all need to keep a list of all the uplifting things we learn as we go through life. Then when we pass on, we can leave some words of wisdom behind for others. I started this writing as a tribute to my mom for all the things she had saved that gave laughter and words of wisdom. I have to say, I found myself laughing at things I have heard several times before, reflecting back on things I have neglected or forgotten, thinking about what has truly made an impression on my life, aging more graciously, how can I bring joy to others more abundantly and what spiritual lessons can I teach others. I too hope that this can bring laughter, some wisdom, some thought provoking subjects, and some fun to you! Share them with friends, post the quotes in places and just enjoy! As, my mom would say, "You don't stop laughing because you grow old, you grow old because you stop laughing!"

She had also written words she wanted read at her funeral which pretty much sums up her spiritual life. "I am at the end of my life and won't see you for a while but the best is yet to come. Jesus has prepared a glorious home for me and all who love him. My mind can't take it all in but I will be waiting for you. Be sure you are coming!" There was another poem she loved and wanted to share it at her funeral. It is as follows: "Do not stand at my grave and weep, I am not there, I do not sleep. I am 1000 winds that blow, I am the diamond glints on the snow. I am the sun on ripened grain, I am the gentle Autumn rain. When you awaken in the morning's hush, I am the swift uplifting rush. Of the quiet birds in circled light, I am the soft star the shines at night. Do not stand at my grave and cry, I am not there; I did not die."

Many times, when we were talking about heaven, I would humorously tell her to be sure and save me a place if she went first, but that thought was always in the future. When the time really came, I still wasn't ready to let her go. When I went to the coffin after the funeral, I wanted to say good bye to her earthly body. I kissed her cheek and took off a ring from my finger and put it on her finger. I knew she wasn't there, but for whatever reason, it gave me some comfort knowing she had something of mine to hold as she was put in her cemetery grave. My tears were for missing her and I always will in this earthly life but I also knew she no longer had pains or the ravages of old age and is in a much better place. I would not wish her back. Someday, I will be with her and I am awaiting that day with anticipation.

I want to end with another prayer that my mom had kept. It is an old Apache Prayer that I really enjoyed reading and I hope you do too!

"May the sun bring you new energy by day. May the moon softly restore you by night. May the rain wash away your worries. May the breeze blow new strength into your being. May you walk gently through the world and know its beauty all the days of your life."

This is a beautiful prayer. After all, we are all in this world together. Most of us want the same things: to live freely, find happiness and joy (whatever that may be for each of us), to find our own spirituality, and to love and be loved. My mom, as well as I, would hope that you all could reach these goals. I wish love, laughter, and longevity to all of you and God Bless!